Special Handball Practice 1 – Step-by-step training of a 3-2-1 defense system

Introduction

Dear reader
Thank you for choosing a book of the handball-uebungen.de training guide series.

The 3-2-1 defense system is an excellent strategy to put the attacking players under pressure in their initial actions. This often results in quick turnovers and fast breaks. However, a good basic fitness as well as a thorough 1-on-1 defense training are prerequisite for this. To make your youth training comprehensive, include practicing the 3-2-1 defense system as a mandatory element.

As in each volume of the handball-uebungen.de series, this book has its focus on practical exercises which can be integrated in each handball training unit. Get inspired, learn how to develop a 3-2-1 defense system, and don't forget to be creative on your own! A short theoretical introduction to the general training schedule will help you to integrate training units into your own annual schedule.

Sample figure:

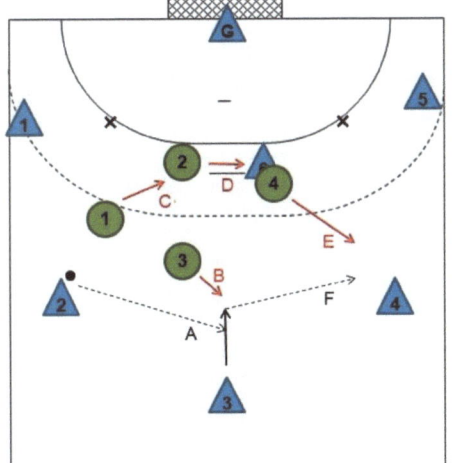

2nd edition (16 Jun 2012)
Published by DV Concept (handball-uebungen.de)
Editors: Jörg Madinger, Elke Lackner
ISBN: 978-3956411519

No reprinting, photomechanical reproduction, storing or processing in electronic systems without the editors' written permission.

Contents

1. Insight into the annual schedule

2. Structuring a training unit

3. Roles/tasks of the coach

4. Key for the training units

5. Training units
   - TU 1: 3-2-1 defense system – Part 1 (★★)
   - TU 2: 3-2-1 defense system – Part 2 (★★)
   - TU 3: 3-2-1 defense system – Part 3 (★★)
   - TU 4: 3-2-1 defense system – Part 4 (★★)
   - TU 5: 3-2-1 defense system – Part 5 (★★)
   - TU 6: 3-2-1 defense system – Part 6 (★★)

6. About the editor

7. Further reference books published by DV Concept

1. Insight into the annual schedule

Training objectives
In the training of **adult teams**, a coach usually will be measured based on his or her success (league position). Hence, the individual training units are strongly focused on the respective opposing team (aim of season). Winning games and making efficient use of the team's potential are paramount.

In the training of **youth teams**, however, the **individual development** is the most important objective which has priority over success. The players should also be trained on a general basis, i.e. on each position (no positional specialization, no offense/defense specialization).

Annual schedule
The following points should be taken into consideration when creating your annual schedule:
- How many training units do I have (do not forget vacations, holidays, and the season schedule)?
- What do I want to achieve/improve this season?
- What goals should be achieved within a given concept (of the club, the association, i.e. the German Handball Association [DHB], for example)? You can refer to the publications of the DHB for information about defense systems, individual offense/defense skills, and the expected performance of a certain age group.
- What skills does my team have (do the individual players have)? You should continuously analyze and document the skills of your team so that you can make a target-performance comparison at a regular basis.

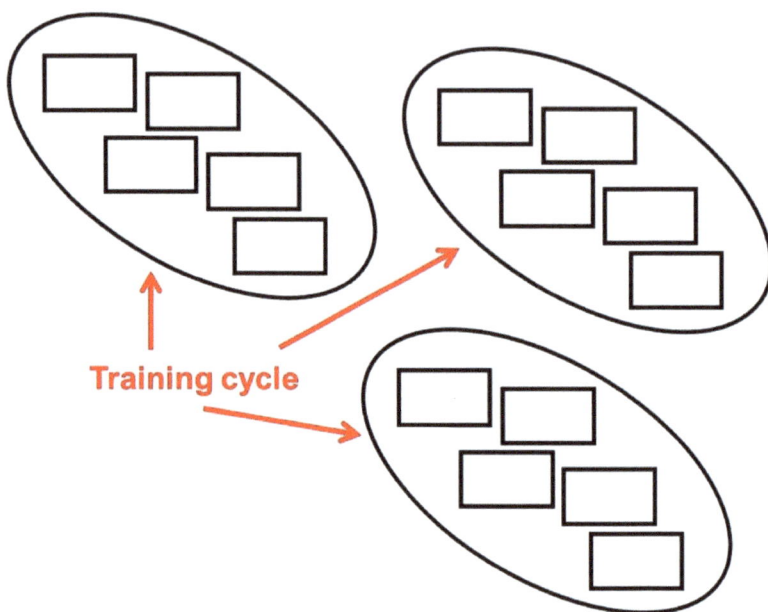

Individual steps of the annual schedule
A handball season can be divided into the following training phases:
- Preparatory phase until the first game: This phase is suitable for improving physical fitness skills such as endurance.
- 1. First part of the season until the Christmas holidays: The Christmas break should be kept in mind here.
- 2. Second part of the season until the end of season.

You should then refine and elaborate these training phases step by step.
- Division of training phases into sections with part-specific objectives (monthly schedule, e.g.)
- Division into weekly schedules
- Planning of individual training units

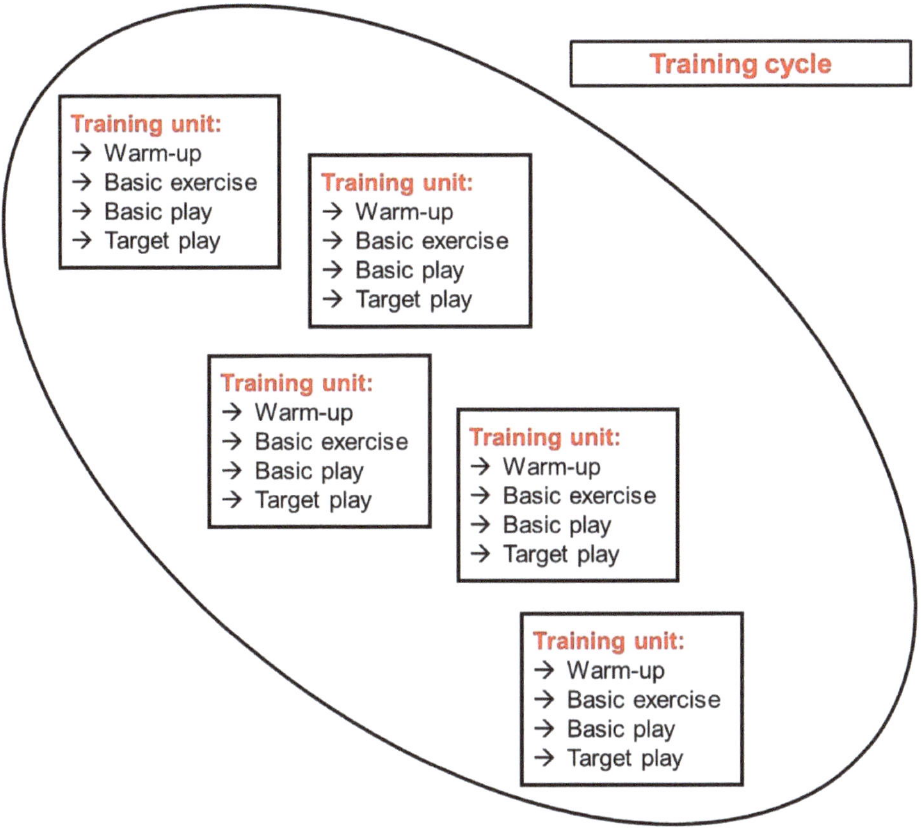

Training cycle

Training unit:
→ Warm-up
→ Basic exercise
→ Basic play
→ Target play

Training unit:
→ Warm-up
→ Basic exercise
→ Basic play
→ Target play

Training unit:
→ Warm-up
→ Basic exercise
→ Basic play
→ Target play

Training unit:
→ Warm-up
→ Basic exercise
→ Basic play
→ Target play

Training unit:
→ Warm-up
→ Basic exercise
→ Basic play
→ Target play

Creating well-structured training units

A clear structure is important for the annual schedule as well as for the planning of the individual training units.

- Work with parts (see monthly schedule). You should work on a special topic over a certain period of time, especially in the training of youth teams. That way, you can repeat exercises and make sure the players memorize the courses.
- Each training unit should have a clear training focus. Do not mix topics within a training unit, but make sure that each exercise has a well-defined objective.
- The players are corrected in accordance with the training unit's focus (when training the defense, defense actions are corrected and pointed out).

2. Structuring a training unit

The focus of the training should run like a red thread through the entire unit. It is advisable to follow the basic timescale below:
- Approx. 10 (15) minutes – warm-up.
- Approx. 20 (30) minutes – basic exercises (2 to 3 exercises max. plus goalkeeper warm-up shooting).
- Approx. 20 (30) minutes – basic play.
- Approx. 10 (15) minutes – target play.

1. timescale for a 60-minute training unit / 2nd timescale in brackets for a 90-minute training unit.

Warm-up practices
- Opening of the training unit: It may be advisable to start the training unit with a ritual (get together in a circle, exchanging high-fives) and to explain the contents and the objectives of the training unit to the players.
- Basic warm-up (jogging, activation of blood circulation and the musculoskeletal system).
- Stretching/strengthening/mobilization (preparing the body for the physical stress of the training unit).
- Short games (these should already focus on the objective of the training unit).

Basic exercises
- Ball familiarization (focused on the objective of the training unit).
- Goalkeeper warm-up shooting (focused on the objective of the training unit).
- Individual technique and tactics training.
- Technique and tactics training in small groups.

In general, the running and passing paths are predefined during the basic exercises (you may increase and vary the requirements during the course of the exercise).

Additional information on basic exercise
- Each player should do the drill (switch quickly).
- Very frequent repetitions.
- The players should rotate or do the drill on both sides simultaneously / slightly delayed to avoid long waiting periods.
- Practice individually (1-on-1 to 2-on-2 max.).
- Add additional tasks/drills, if applicable (to make the exercise more complex).

Basic play

Most of all, the basic play differs from the basic exercise in such a way that now there are several **options for action** (decisions). The player(s) should realize the respective options and make the ideal decision. Here, the players practice decision-making in particular.
- The players should now implement what they practiced during the basic exercises under **competitive conditions**.
- Working with alternative actions – practicing the decision-making process.
- The players should repeat the drill frequently and try out different actions.
- Working in small groups (3-on-3 to 4-on-4 max.).

Target play
- The players now implement what they practice before in free play. To increase their motivation, you may award additional points or additional attacks for correct implementation.
- In the target play, the players implement what they practiced before (5-on-5, 6-on-6).

Depending on the contents and the objectives of the training unit, you may have to slightly adjust the timescales of the basic exercise and basic play (e.g. for endurance training where they may be substituted by endurance units).

Set topics
- Individual training of the players according to the respective conceptual training framework (DHB or the club's individual conceptual framework).
- Tactical training of defense and offense systems (age-dependent):
    o From man coverage to a 6-0 defense system, for example.
    o From 1-on1 to 6-on-6 with initial actions practiced in teams, for example.

Choose topic of training unit:
→ Red thread

Warm up:
Time:
- approx. 10 (15) minutes

Practices:
- "Playful warm-up"
- Games
- Coordination runs
- (Stretching and strengthening)

Basic exercise:
Time:
- approx. 20 (30) minutes

Characteristics:
- Individual/Small groups

Practices:
- Exact instructions re. course of the exercise
- Variants with exact instructions re. the course
- From simple to complex
- No waiting periods for players

Basic play:
Time:
- approx. 20 (30) minutes

Characteristics:
- Small groups

Practices:
- Exact instructions re. course
- Competition

Target play:
Time:
- approx. 10 (15) minutes

Characteristics:
- Team play (small groups)

Practices:
- Free play with the contents of the basic exercise and basic play
- Competition

3. Roles/tasks of the coach

It is mainly the personality and the behavior of the coach that makes the training a success. Therefore, it is important to observe certain behavioral rules to guarantee a successful training. The coach's social skills have an impact as important as his expertise.

A coach should:
- describe the training and its objectives to his team at the beginning of the training unit
- always speak loud and clear
- talk from such a position that all players can hear his instructions and corrections
- recognize and correct mistakes and give advice when correcting
- mainly correct what is part of the training objective
- point out and compliment on individual progress (give the player self-confidence)
- support and permanently challenge the players
- always be a role model - during training and games, but also outside the court
- come to training and games well-prepared and in a timely manner

4. Key for the training units:

✖	Cone
⦿	Ball box
▲1	Attacking player
●1	Defense player
▬	Small gym mat
▬	Large safety mat
◾	Small vaulting box
━	Foam noodles (foam beams)
☐	Small vaulting box (upside down)
○	Hoop
CF/CB	Defense player: Center front/center back

Difficulty level:

★ Simple requirement (all youth and adult teams)
★★ Intermediate requirement (youth teams under 15 years of age and adult teams)
★★★ Higher requirement (youth teams under 17 years of age and adult teams)
★★★★ Highest requirement (competitive area)

Special Handball Practice 1 – Step-by-step training of a 3-2-1 defense system

5. Training units

No.: Def. 1	Topic: 3-2-1 defense system			★★	90
Opening part		**Main part**			
X	Warm-up/Stretching		Offense/Individual		Jumping power
	Running exercise		Offense/Small groups		Sprint contest
X	Short game		Offense/Team		Goalkeeper
	Coordination		Offense/Series of shots		
	Coordination run	X	Defense/Individual		**Final part**
	Strengthening	X	Defense/Small groups	X	Closing game
X	Ball familiarization		Defense/Team		Final sprint
X	Goalkeeper warm-up shooting		Athletics		
			Endurance		

Equipment required:
- 8 cones
- Sufficient number of handballs

No.: 1-1	Warm-up/Stretching	15	15

Course:
- Two players crisscross the court and keep passing a handball.
- Change running moves constantly (forward, backward, sidestep).
- Jump shot passes.
- Passing with the non-throwing hand.
- Crossing.
- The players perform stretching exercises individually/together.

No.: 1-2	Short game	10	25

Course:
- Two teams play team ball in the playing field.
- After each pass (A), the players must run around a cone first (B) before they may receive a pass again.
- Without dribbling.

Variants:
- The players must not play return passes.
- Jump shot passes.
- Passing with the non-throwing hand.

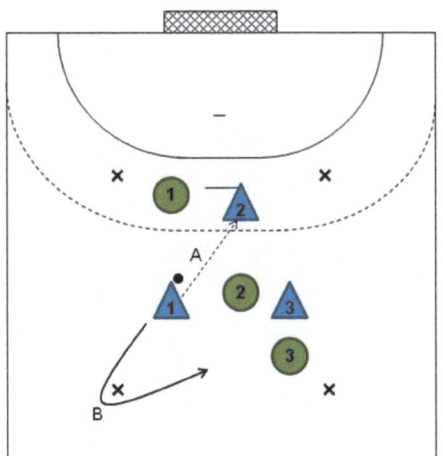

| No.: 1-3 | Ball familiarization | 10 | 35 |

Course:

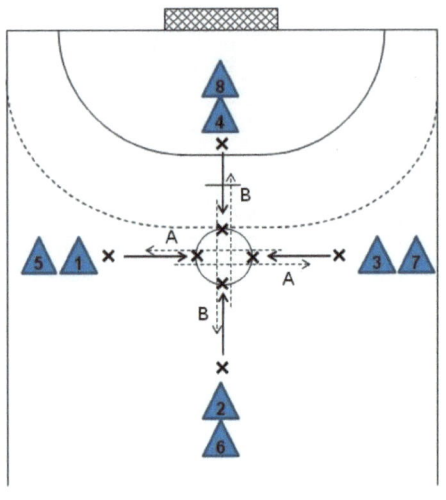

- 1 makes a piston movement towards the cone in the front and passes (A) the ball to 3 who also starts the piston movement.
- Simultaneously, 2 makes a piston movement towards the cone in the front and passes (B) the ball to 4 who also starts the piston movement.
- As soon as 1 has passed the ball, he quickly moves back to the right side and lines up behind 2.
- 2 lines up behind 3, and so on.

Variants:

- 1 runs to 3 in a semicircle curve (to the opposite side) after the pass and lines up there. 2 lines up behind 4, 3 lines up behind 1, and 4 lines up behind 2.
- The players move back until they are able to do the piston movement towards the first (backmost) cone and pass the ball to the other group from this position -> longer passing path.

| No.: 1-4 | Goalkeeper warm-up shooting | 10 | 45 |

Course:

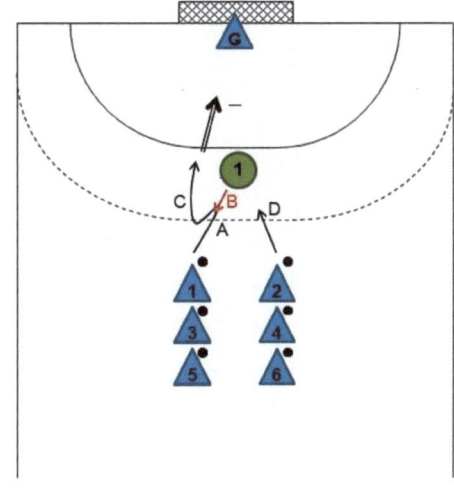

- **1** starts to run with the ball and lifts his arm for a shot (A).
- **1** dynamically steps forward towards **1** and pushes him back in the usual defending manner (about half a meter) (B).
- **1** moves back to his initial position after the action against **1**.
- After **1** has been pushed back, he approaches the goal and shoots as instructed (hands, top, bottom, middle) (C).
- Now **2** starts the same course on the other side (D).

⚠ Make sure that **1** maintains the correct defense posture (attacking the throwing hand and the diagonal hip).

⚠ The players should give **1** enough time so that he can move back to his initial position.

⚠ **1** should push back the attacking player dynamically rather than tackling him.

Special Handball Practice 1 – Step-by-step training of a 3-2-1 defense system

No.: 1-5	Defense/Individual		10	55

Course:

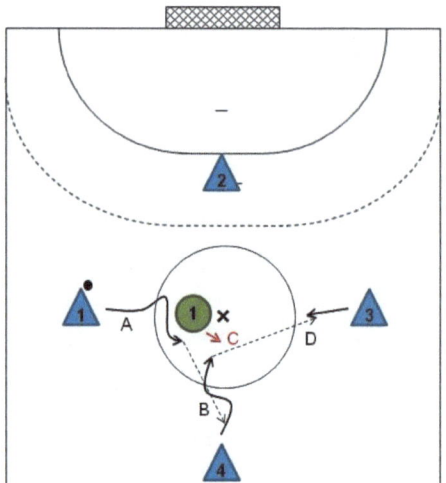

- ▲1 starts a 1-on-1 action against ●1, tries to step into the circle with the ball, and touch the cone in the center (A).
- If ▲1 is being tackled or cannot move any further, he passes the ball to ▲4 (or ▲2; passing to the opposite player is not allowed) (B).
- ●1 dynamically moves to the next attacking player with quick steps (C) and defends against the action of ▲4.
- If ▲4 cannot move any further (or has touched the cone), he passes the ball to the next attacking player (D).
- The players keep playing until ●1 has performed eight defense actions. After this, change the defense player.

⚠ ●1 should be given enough time to take up the correct defense posture before the attacking players start their action.

Special Handball Practice 1 – Step-by-step training of a 3-2-1 defense system

No.: 1-6	Defense/Small groups	10	65

Course:

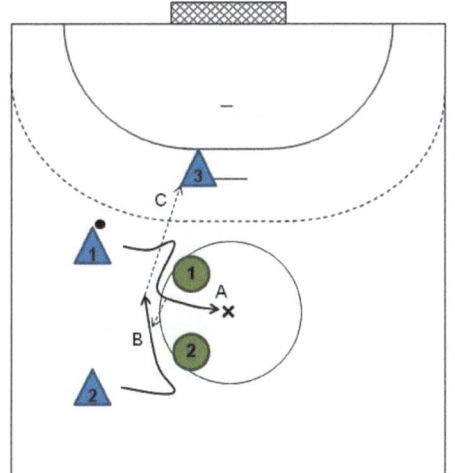

- 1 and 2 try to play off 1 and 2 in such a way that they can touch the cone in the center (A and B).
- 3 serves as feeder/receiver (C).
- If 1 and 2 have been tackled (cannot move any further), they move back immediately and start the next action at once (five actions in a row in total; afterwards, the players switch tasks).

⚠ 1 and 2 should keep trying to break through to the cone, also by performing 1-on-1 actions.

⚠ Suspend the double dribble rule; the attacking players should perform several actions in a row in order to challenge 1 and 2 vigorously.

| No.: 1-7 | Defense/Small groups | 15 | 80 |

Initial position:

- ▲1 starts the piston movement with the ball.
- ●1 stands in an offensive defense position.
- ●2 stands defensively and covers ▲6.
- ▲6 is allowed to move within the zone between the cones.

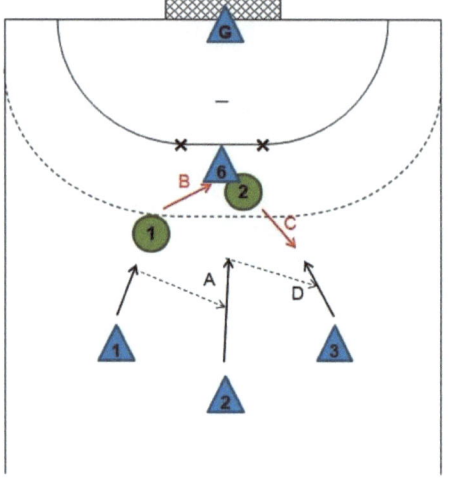

Figure 1

Course:

- ▲1 makes a piston movement and passes the ball into the running path of ▲2 (A).
- ●1 moves back and takes over ▲6 (B).
- ▲2 makes a piston movement, passes the ball to ▲3 into his running path (D), and immediately moves back to his initial position (center back).
- ●2 offensively makes a step forward and attacks ▲3 (C) (figure 2).
- ▲3 may now try to pass the ball to ▲6. If this is not possible, he passes the ball back to ▲2.
- And so on.

⚠ ▲6 should keep his position during the first actions. During the further course of the exercise, he may start to move more vigorously within the zone between the cones.

⚠ Adjust the distance between the cones to the players' level of performance.

⚠ ●1 and ●2 should do quick steps and try to prevent passes to ▲6 for as long as possible.

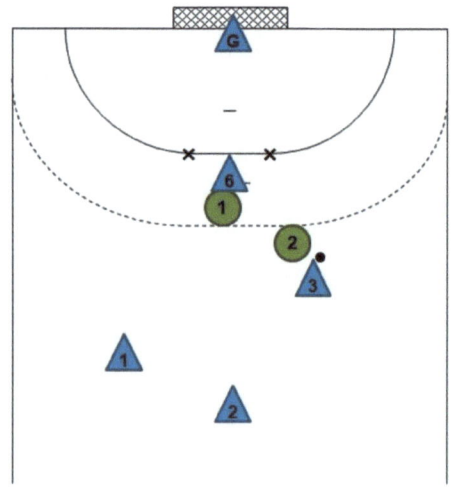

Figure 2

Special Handball Practice 1 – Step-by-step training of a 3-2-1 defense system

No.: 1-8	Closing game	10	90

Course:
- Make two teams. Both teams play handball against each other.

Instructions:
- Offensive defense at 9 to 10 meters without fixed man coverage. As soon as an attacking player enters this zone, he will be covered (followed) by one of the defense players.

 The defense players should communicate permanently and agree upon who is in charge of the respective attacking player.

⚠ The players should use their arms and hold their opponents in front of them.

No.: Def. 2	Topic: 3-2-1 defense system			★★	90
Opening part		**Main part**			
X	Warm-up/Stretching		Offense/Individual		Jumping power
	Running exercise		Offense/Small groups	X	Sprint contest
X	Short game		Offense/Team		Goalkeeper
	Coordination		Offense/Series of shots		
	Coordination run	X	Defense/Individual	**Final part**	
	Strengthening		Defense/Small groups	X	Closing game
X	Ball familiarization		Defense/Team		Final sprint
X	Goalkeeper warm-up shooting		Athletics		
			Endurance		

Equipment required:
- 2 cones per player
- 2 ball boxes, each with a sufficient number of handballs

No.: 2-1	Warm-up/Stretching	15	15

Course:
- The players make pairs. One player runs in the front and does a running movement (forward, backward, sidestep) which the other player must do as well. The players switch tasks after a couple of minutes.
- The players pass a ball easily while crisscrossing the court.
- Afterwards, the players perform stretching exercises together; one player does an exercise which the other players must do as well.

No.: 2-2	Short game		10	25

Course:

Make teams in such a way that there is an outnumbered situation (example: five attacking players and three defense players).

- The five attacking players pass the ball (A).
- The three defending players must try to touch the player in ball possession by doing quick steps (B).
- Change the players after a couple of minutes.
- Without dribbling.

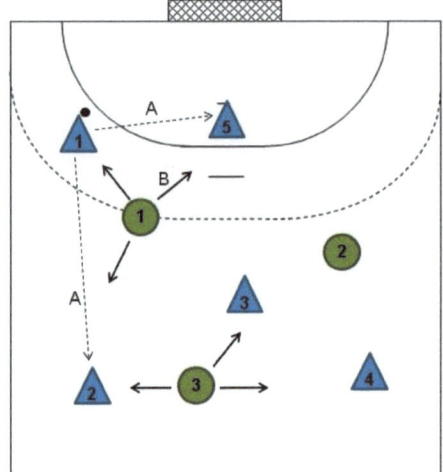

Task:

- The attacking players try to play 10 passes without being touched. If they succeed, the defending players must do 10 push-ups, for example. If they fail, the attacking players must do 10 push-ups.

Variants:

- Dribbling is allowed.
- No return passes.
- Jump shot passes.
- Passing with the non-throwing hand.

| No.: 2-3 | Ball familiarization | 10 | 35 |

Course A:
- The player keeps sidestepping on the "8 path" around the cones and receives passes from ▲ over and over again.

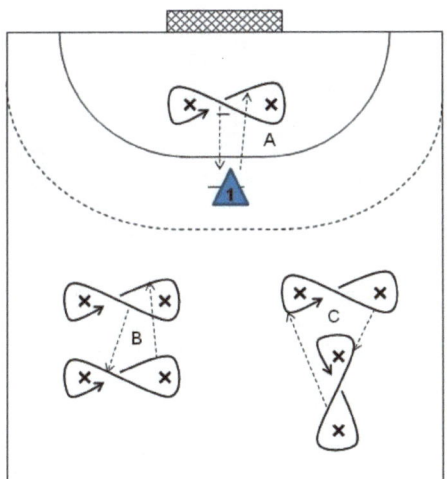

Course B:
- Both players sidestep (same direction) on the "8 path" around the cones while passing a ball.

Variants:
- Opposite running direction.
- Changing the running direction on command while constantly passing the ball.

Course C:
- 1 player sidesteps on the "8 path" around the cones while the second player runs forward and backward on the "8 path"; both keep passing the ball.

Variants:
- Chest passes.
- Increase the passing and running speed step by step.

| No.: 2-4 | Sprint contest | 5 | 40 |

Course:

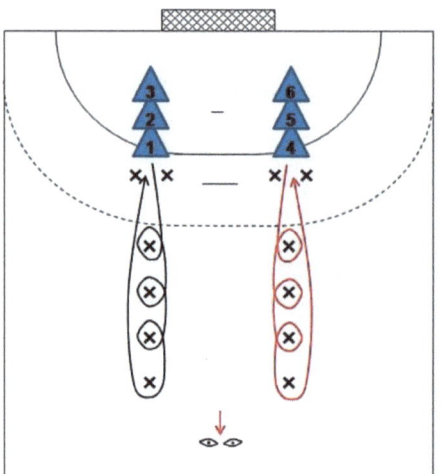

- ▲1 and ▲4 start in parallel on command. They sprint to the respective first cone and run around it one time, while maintaining the same viewing direction.
- Afterwards, they sprint to the next cone, around the fourth cone and then back in forward direction (viewing direction to their group). Finally, they exchange a high-five with the player who is about to start next.
- And so on.

The losing team must do push-ups or sit-ups, for example.

Variants:

- Change the viewing direction (sidesteps).
- Dribble a ball during the drill.

| No.: 2-5 | Goalkeeper warm-up shooting | 10 | 50 |

Course:

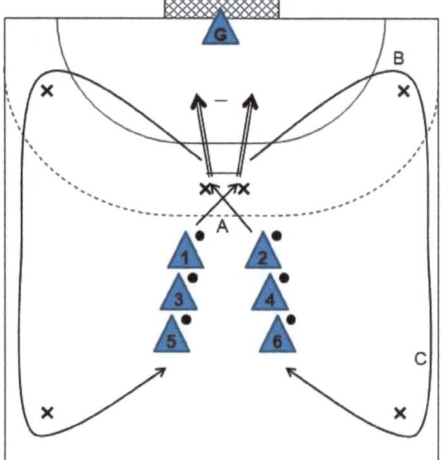

- ▲1 starts to run dynamically and does a jump shot next to the cones (A). Afterwards, ▲2 starts from the right side.
- Players who start on the right side shoot at the left side of the goal, as instructed (top, middle, bottom); players who start on the left side shoot at the right side of the goal, as instructed (top, middle, bottom).
- The players should quickly start and shoot one after another.
- After the shot, the shooting players sprint to the cone in the corner (B) and around the cone near the center line (C).

Special Handball Practice 1 – Step-by-step training of a 3-2-1 defense system

Variants:
- First shot at the goalkeeper's hands, then at the top, bottom, and middle of the goal.
- Shooting decision: Top or bottom, but always both approach the goal and shoot diagonally.

No.: 2-6	Defense/Individual	10	60

Setting:
- The players make pairs and spread throughout the court, each pair having a cone (but initially without a ball).

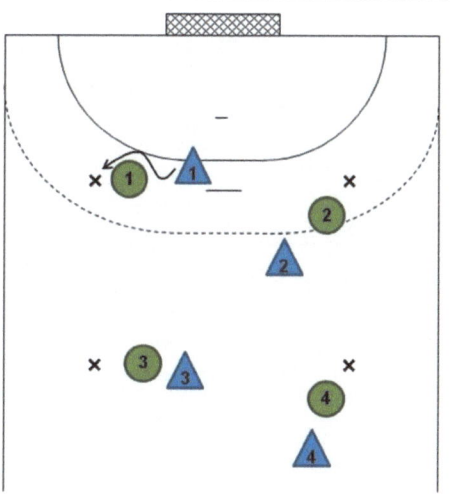

Course of the 1st round:
- ① defends the cone against ▲ and obstructs the way to the cone by quickly sidestepping and moving forward.
- ▲ performs five actions in a row trying to approach the cone without a ball. If he is not able to break through, or if he has been tackled, he moves back a bit and starts the next action at once, without a break.
- After five actions, the two players switch tasks.

Course of the 2st round:
- ▲ does the same course as above, but now **with** a ball. He dribbles towards ①, picks up the ball, and tries to play off his opponent using a body feint. If he does not succeed, he immediately moves back a bit and starts the next action, without a break.

⚠ The players should perform the five actions in a highly dynamic manner; afterwards, they may have a break.

⚠ Make sure that the players maintain the correct defense posture, i.e. attacking the throwing hand and the diagonal hip.

| No.: 2-7 | Defense/Individual | 10 | 70 |

Course:

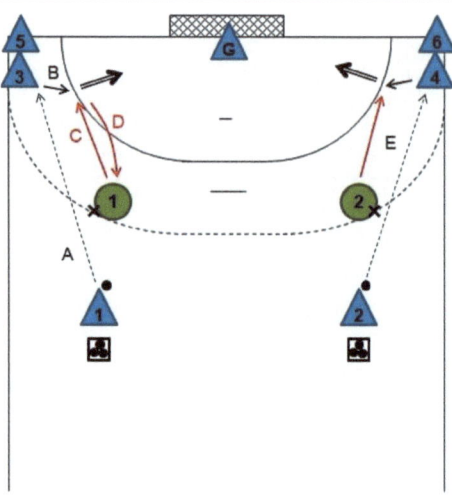

- ① and ② stand in the initial position next to the cone at the 9-meter line.
- As soon as 🔺 has passed the ball to 🔺 on the wing position (A), ① quickly moves to the wing position (C) to prevent 🔺 from shooting / to interrupt the shot (B).
- Following the action, ① moves back to the cone again (D).
- Afterwards, repeat the course on the right side (E).
- And so on.

⚠ ① should be given the chance to interrupt 🔺 approaching the goal by quickly moving to the wing position.

⚠ ① might be given the chance to move to the wing position earlier (when 🔺 picks up a ball from the ball box, and not only after he played the pass, for example).

Special Handball Practice 1 – Step-by-step training of a 3-2-1 defense system

No.: 2-8	Defense/Individual	10	80

Course:

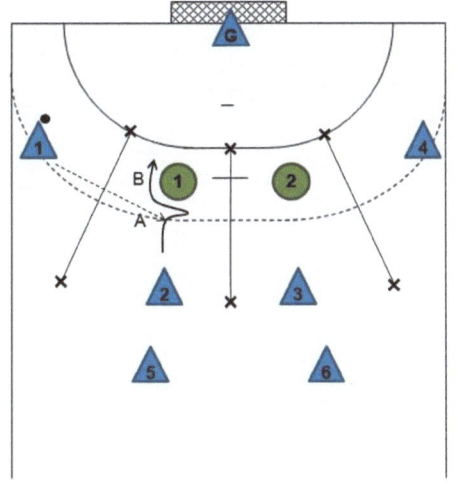

- 2 plays 1-on-1 (B) against 1 in a confined playing field. 1 and 3 support him as feeders/receivers (A).
- After the action, 3 starts and also plays 1-on-1 against 2. 5 and 4 support him as feeders/receivers.
- Afterwards, it is the turn of 5 and 6. The attacking players and the feeders/receivers should always switch tasks.

⚠️ 1 and 2 should quickly step forward and to the side in order to interrupt the attacking player while he does a body feint.

⚠️ The defense players should act rather than react.

⚠️ Highly dynamic, no break between the individual actions.

⚠️ The defense players should be corrected permanently (basic posture, legwork, arm posture).

No.: 2-9	Closing game	10	90

Course:
- Make two teams. Both teams play handball against each other.

Instructions:
- Offensive defense at 9 to 10 meters without fixed man coverage. As soon as an attacking player enters this zone, he will be covered (followed) by one of the defense players.

⚠️ The defense players should communicate permanently and agree upon who is in charge of the respective attacking player.

⚠️ The players should use their arms and hold their opponents in front of them.

No.: Def. 3	Topic: 3-2-1 defense system			★★	90
Opening part		**Main part**			
X	Warm-up/Stretching		Offense/Individual		Jumping power
	Running exercise		Offense/Small groups		Sprint contest
X	Short game		Offense/Team		Goalkeeper
	Coordination		Offense/Series of shots		
	Coordination run	X	Defense/Individual		**Final part**
	Strengthening	X	Defense/Small groups	X	Closing game
X	Ball familiarization		Defense/Team		Final sprint
X	Goalkeeper warm-up shooting		Athletics		
			Endurance		

Equipment required:
- 2 small vaulting boxes, upside down
- 1 cone per player (at least 4 cones)
- 2 large safety mats, sufficient number of handballs

No.: 3-1	Warm-up/Stretching	15	15

Course:
- 2 to 3 players make teams having one ball per team. The teams crisscross the court while passing the ball.
- They should change their running direction repeatedly, whereas the player in ball possession (dribbles a few meters) defines the running direction (forward, backward, sidestep) and the two other players follow him.

- The players perform stretching exercises together.

No.: 3-2	Short game		10	25

Course:
- Make two teams. Both teams play team ball against each other.

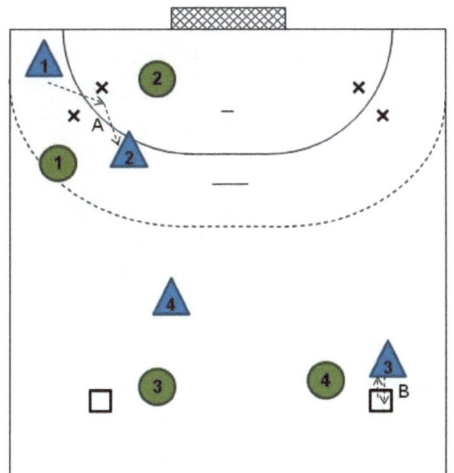

Teams may score points by:

Either: ▲1 plays a bounce pass through the cone goal in such a way that a teammate can catch the ball (A).

Or: ▲3 throws the ball into the box in such a way that he can catch it again (B).

Each team defends one cone goal and one box.

Exercise/objective:
- The attacking players try to score 10 points. If they succeed, the defending players must do 10 push-ups, for example.
- The players must adjust quickly, if a goal is covered by an opponent.

Variants:
- Allow dribbling.
- No return passes allowed (for larger groups).
- Jump shot passes.
- Passing with the non-throwing hand.
- Do not assign the goals; the players can score points randomly.
- The players can only score a point, if they hit both "goals" (cone and box) one after another.

| No.: 3-3 | Ball familiarization | 10 | 35 |

Course:
- ▲2 passes the ball to the left to ▲1 (A) and runs to the right (B) until he has reached the player he formerly passed the ball to.
- ▲1 passes the ball to the left to ▲3 (C) and runs to the right (D) until he has reached the position he passed the ball to.
- And so on.

Variants:
- Change the passing and running direction.
- On command, the players should change the passing/running direction at once (quick adjustment and instant implementation).

⚠ The players should be careful not to crash into each other while running.

| No.: 3-4 | Goalkeeper warm-up shooting | 10 | 45 |

Course:
- ▲1 passes the ball to ●1 and receives a return pass into his running path.
- ▲1 now plays 1-on-1 against ●1 and tries to break through on the right side (A).
- ●1 defends against the body/throwing hand and pushes ▲1 further to the right (B).
- ▲1 passes the ball into the running path of ▲2 (C). ▲2 runs to the right and around the cone, and eventually shoots at the short goalpost, as instructed (top, middle, bottom) (D).
- The goalkeeper must not stand next to the goalpost in the beginning but rather keep a certain distance and then try to save the shot (E).
- After passing the ball to ▲2 (C), ▲1 immediately moves to the left (F).

Special Handball Practice 1 – Step-by-step training of a 3-2-1 defense system

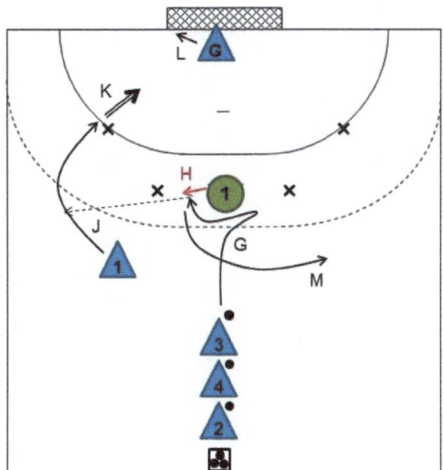

- After **1** has passed the ball to **2**, **3** starts his action.
- **3** passes the ball to **1** and receives a return pass into his running path.
- **3** now plays 1-on-1 against **1** and tries to break through on the left side (G).
- **1** defends against the body/throwing hand and pushes **3** further to the left (H).
- **3** passes the ball into the running path of **1** (J). **1** runs to the left and around the cone, and eventually shoots at the short goalpost, as instructed (top, middle, bottom) (K).
- The goalkeeper again should move towards the ball almost from the center of the goal (L).
- After passing the ball to **1** (J), **3** immediately runs to the right side (M). And so on.

⚠ The course should be timed in such a way that the goalkeeper has enough time to get back into his initial position after each shot.

⚠ **1** should defend against the attacking players in a highly dynamic manner, but allow the pass.

Basic course:
- After the shot on the wing position (D and K), the players should run back immediately, pick up a new ball, and line up again so that the defending player and the goalkeeper face a long series of attacks and shots.

Special Handball Practice 1 – Step-by-step training of a 3-2-1 defense system

| No.: 3-5 | Defense/Individual | 10 | 55 |

Objective:
- Dynamic defense movement (stepping forward) towards the attacking player and moving back again (triangle movement).

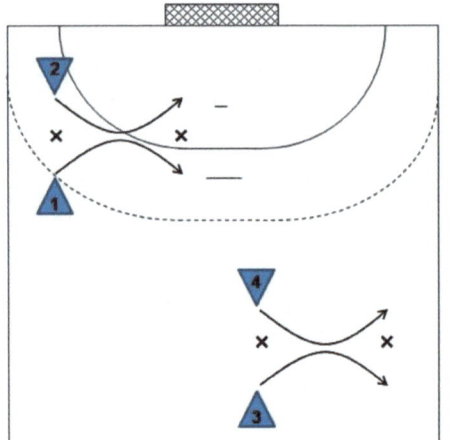

Setting:
- Put the two cones on the floor with a distance of 5 meters in between. The two players stand at the cones with a distance of about 1.5 meters.

Course:
In alternate order, one player is the attacking player, the other one performs the defense action (the tasks may be switched either after each action, or one player does all the defense actions in a row):

- Round 1: ▲1 is the attacking player and runs forward. ▲2 is the defense player, makes a step forward towards the attacking player, and pushes him back dynamically with both hands (the running energy should be neutralized by pushing the attacking player back slightly; hard pushing is not allowed!). Afterwards, both players move back to the opposite side and start the drill over.
- Round 2: ▲1 has a ball; he should feint a shot (lift his arm) during the piston movement. ▲2 dynamically defends against the attacking player's throwing hand and hip, and pushes ▲1 back.
- Round 3: Now, ▲1 feints a jump shot, which ▲2 should block by defending against the attacking player's throwing hand/shoulder.

Repetitions:
- The players perform 5 to 10 actions each on the left and right side. Afterwards, they may take a break. They should repeat the overall course 2 to 5 times in total.

Defense player hand/arm posture:
- One hand must be positioned in direction of the attacking player's throwing hand, the other hand in direction of the attacking player's hip.

⚠ The defense players should alternately push the attacking player back (no foul) and tackle him (block both arms so that the attacking player is unable to perform any further actions = foul).

⚠ The attacking player should also use his other arm for the shooting feint (but inform the defense player beforehand).

⚠ The attacking players should approach the defense player not always in the same way but rather modify their moves (a bit more to the left/right, slightly bent ...).

⚠ **Make sure that the players have enough breaks; the drill is very exhausting.**

No.: 3-6	Defense/Small groups	10	65

Course:

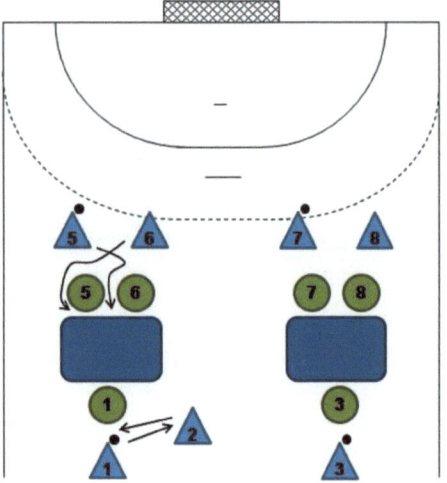

- Two groups (each two attacking players (5 and 6) and two defense players (5 und 6)) play against each other at one mat. Their aim is to lay the ball down on the mat.
- The attacking players always perform five actions in a row. If they have been tackled or fouled, they should move back immediately and start over.
- If there are not enough players, one of the groups should play 1-on-1 (3 and 3) or with a feeder/receiver (1, 1 and 2).

Group change:
- Switch tasks after five attacks (the defense players become the attacking players).
- Change the group pairings to create new challenges.

Important for the defense players:

⚠ They should always stand in line and avoid being pulled apart horizontally.

⚠ They should step forward towards the attacking players vigorously and push them back.

⚠ They should communicate/talk loudly.

⚠ They should hand/take over.

Important for the attacking players:

⚠ The attacking players should vigorously seek physical contact instead of playing at distance.

⚠ They should approach the mat 1-on-1 or by crossing.

| No.: 3-7 | Defense/Small groups | 15 | 80 |

Setting:
- 2 and 3 play 2-on-2 against 1 and 2; 1 and 4 serve as feeders/receivers (A).

Course 1 (figure 1):
- 2 and 3 try to play off the two defense players through dynamic piston movements and by performing 1-on-1 actions (B or C).
- If the attacking players cannot move any further or have been tackled, they move back immediately and start the action over.
- The attacking players should keep their positions, i.e. they should play without crossing.
- As soon as one of the players has shot at the goal, the next two attacking players may start.
- Change the defense players at regular intervals.

Course 2 (figure 2):
- 2 and 3 try to get into a good shooting position by crossing (F) after receiving a pass from the feeders (E).

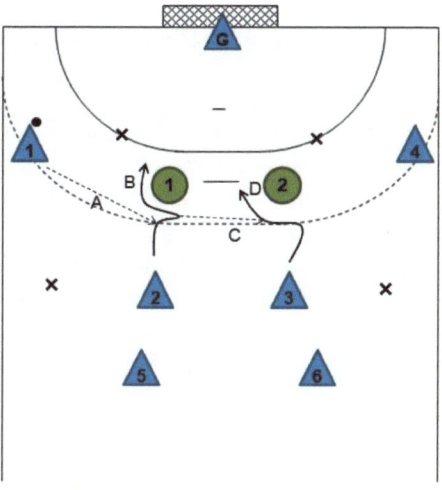

Figure 1

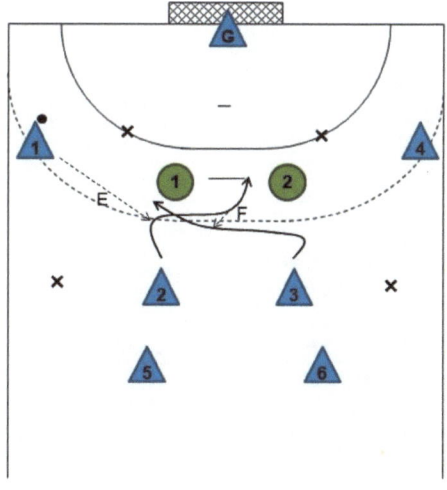

Figure 2

⚠ The attacking players should approach the defense line dynamically after a maximum of 1 to 2 passes, and try to shoot at the goal.

⚠ The defense players should step forward dynamically towards the attacking players and interrupt them.

⚠ 1 and 2 should communicate permanently during the attacking players' crossing moves and organize the handing over.

Special Handball Practice 1 – Step-by-step training of a 3-2-1 defense system

No.: 3-8	Closing game	10	90

Course:
- Make two teams. Both teams play handball against each other.

Instructions:
- Man coverage beginning at the center line, not fixed. Depending on the respective position, the defense players should agree upon who is in charge of and/or who will take over which attacking player (the players should avoid running around haphazardly and searching their opponent).
- If a team manages to steal the ball and directly score a goal, they may play another attack starting from their own half of the court.

 The players should use their arms and hold their opponents in front of them.

Define an extra task for the losing team (e.g. accelerating run plus push-ups/sit-ups).

No.: Def. 4		Topic: 3-2-1 defense system		★★	90
Opening part		**Main part**			
X	Warm-up/Stretching		Offense/Individual		Jumping power
	Running exercise		Offense/Small groups	X	Sprint contest
X	Short game		Offense/Team		Goalkeeper
	Coordination		Offense/Series of shots		
	Coordination run		Defense/Individual		**Final part**
	Strengthening	X	Defense/Small groups		Closing game
X	Ball familiarization	X	Defense/Team		Final sprint
X	Goalkeeper warm-up shooting		Athletics		
			Endurance		

Equipment required:
- 6 small gym mats
- 6 cones
- About 5 foam beams (or one coordination ladder)
- 7 hoops
- 2 ball boxes, each with a sufficient number of handballs

No.: 4-1	Warm-up/Stretching	15	15

Course:
- Two players each jog through the court together and pass a ball.
- They should change their running direction (forward, backward, sidestep) and running moves (hopping, sidestepping, bending the knees) constantly.
- Normal passes/jump shot passes, passes with the non-throwing hand.
- Imitating; i.e. One player makes a certain move, which the other one must copy.
- Afterwards, the players perform stretching exercises together; one player does an exercise which the others must do as well.

Special Handball Practice 1 – Step-by-step training of a 3-2-1 defense system

| No.: 4-2 | Short game | 10 | 25 |

Course:
- The players get a point, if they manage to play a pass to their teammate standing on the mat (A).
- They do not get the point, if a player of the other team touches the mat (B). In this case, the players keep playing.
- Dribbling is allowed.

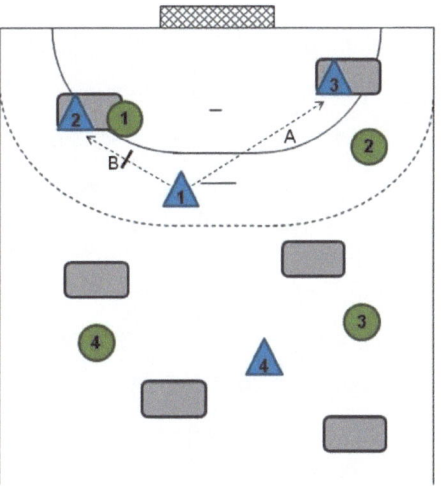

Exercise/objective:
- The attacking players try to score 10 points. If they succeed, the defending players must do 10 push-ups, for example.
- The players are not allowed to play passes from one mat to another mat; they must leave the mat first.

Variants:
- Without dribbling.
- No return passes.
- Jump shot passes.
- Passing with the non-throwing hand.

| No.: 4-3 | Ball familiarization | | 10 | 35 |

Course:

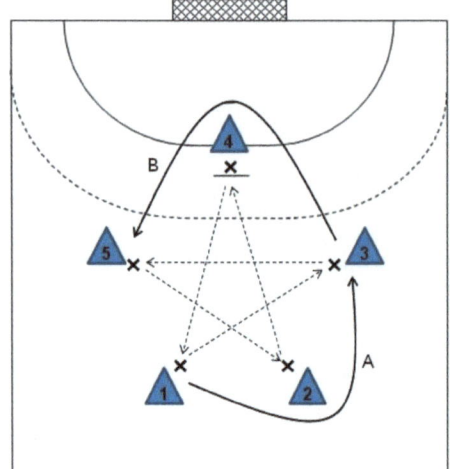

- The players should always skip the next position: 1 passes to 3, 3 passes to 5, 5 passes to 2, 2 passes to 4, and so on.
- The players line up behind the player who received their pass; however, they should run around the other players (1 passes to 3 and runs around 2 (A) in order to line up behind 3).
- 3 passes to 5, runs around 4 (B), and lines up behind 5.

Variant:

- 2nd ball (1 and 2 each have a ball and start the course simultaneously).
- Run and pass the ball to the right/left.
- Pass the ball to the right and run to the left, and vice versa (highly dynamic!).

Special Handball Practice 1 – Step-by-step training of a 3-2-1 defense system

| No.: 4-4 | Sprint contest | 5 | 40 |

Course:

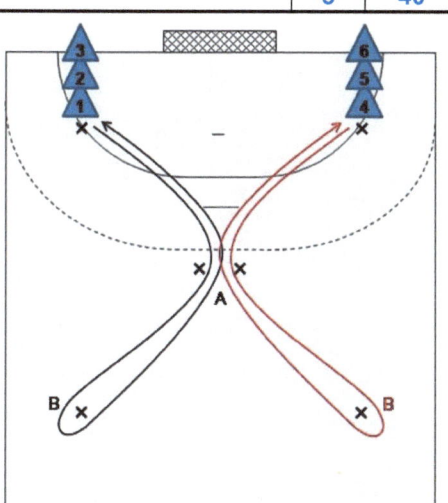

- 1 and 4 start in parallel on the coach's command. They sprint through the narrow cone goal (A), run a curve around the outer cone (B) and back again.
- They exchange a high-five with the player who is about to start next.
- And so on.

The losing team must do push-ups or sit-ups, for example.

⚠ As the cone goal in the center is very narrow, the players should be careful not to crash when running through. However, the distance between the cones must not be too long either. The players should be able to compete fairly when running through the narrow gap.

Variants:

- Dribble a ball during the drill.

| No.: 4-5 | Goalkeeper warm-up shooting | 10 | 50 |

Course:
- All players stand in front of the hoops, each player holding a ball.
- They do quick steps and touch the ground only one time per hoop (A).
- Afterwards, they sprint around the cones (B) and towards the foam beams. They run through the line of foam beams with two steps per interspace (left/right) (C).
- Afterwards, they shoot at the goal, as instructed.

Variant:
- Position the hoops in a different order again and again.
- Change the instructions regarding floor contact/steps when the players run through the line of foam beams. However, make sure that there is a smooth flow; the goalkeeper should face a quick series of shots.

| No.: 4-6 | Defense/Small groups | | 12 | 62 |

Course:

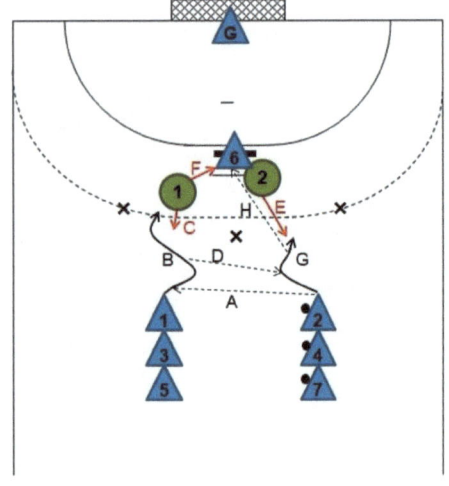

- 🔺1 makes a piston movement and receives the ball from 🔺2 into his running path (A).
- 🔺1 tries to get past 🟢1 1-on-1 (B) – who makes a step forward (C) – and to shoot at the goal. 🔺2 should avoid a pass to the pivot.
- If 🔺1 cannot break through, he passes the ball to 🔺2 into his running path (D).
- 🟢2 makes a step forward (E) and tries to defend against 🔺2 1-on-1 (G).
- 🟢1 quickly moves back to the pivot (F) in order to avoid a pass from 🔺2 (H).
- If 🔺2 can neither break through nor pass the ball to the pivot, he passes back to 🔺1; 🟢1 makes a step forward again and 🟢2 must move back to the pivot.
- As soon as the attacking players have shot at the goal, or the defending players have stolen the ball, 🔺3 and 🔺4 start the drill over as new attacking players.

⚠️ 🟢1 and 🟢2 should move back to the pivot quickly after the 1-on-1 action.

⚠️ The pivot initially stands on a foam beam at the 6-meter line. He must always keep one foot on the foam beam. During the further course of the drill, the pivot may move more and more freely.

⚠️ 🟢1 and 🟢2 should clearly communicate with each other.

| No.: 4-7 | Defense/Small groups | 13 | 75 |

Basic setting:
- 3-on-3 play.

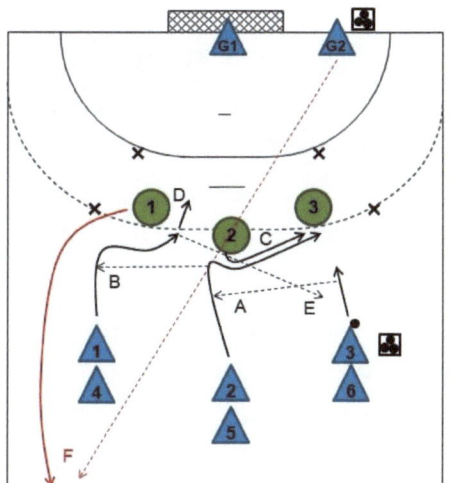

Course:

- ③ makes a piston movement and passes the ball into the running path of ② (A).
- ② makes a piston movement slightly to the left and passes the ball to ① into his running path (B). After the pass, ② dynamically runs in the opposite direction and tries to get past ② and to the 6-meter line.
- ② obstructs the path and prevents ② from moving towards the 6-meter line using his arms actively (C). ② stays in the front and hands over ② to ③ (moves along with him).
- ① may now decide whether he should try to get past ① 1-on-1 (D) or if he should pass the ball to ③ (E).
- Afterwards, the attacking team should keep on playing creatively and try to score a goal.
- If the defense players manage to steal the ball or to tackle the attacking ball holder, the teams switch tasks.
- ①, ②, and ③ immediately start a fast break and sprint until they have crossed the center line. The foremost player (i.e. the player who runs an ideal path) receives a pass from the goalkeeper and eventually shoots at the goal (F).
- ①, ②, and ③ become the new defense players.

⚠ ② must obstruct the path in order to tackle ② and to prevent him from breaking through.

⚠ The respective defense player should force/push ② away by using his arms.

| No.: 4-8 | Defense/Team | 15 | 90 |

Course:

- 5 passes to 2 (A).
- 3 makes a step forward and attacks 2 (B).
- 2 covers 6 in parallel (C).
- 1 simultaneously stands offensively at the 9-meter line, between 1 and 4 (D).
- 2 passes the ball into the running path of 3 (E).
- 3 passes the ball into the running path of 1 (K).
- 2 dynamically makes a step forward and attacks 1 (F) in parallel.
- 3 takes over 6 in parallel (G).
- 1 dynamically runs to the wing position and blocks 4 (H).
- Figure 3 shows the positions when the left back player is in ball possession.
- 4 secures the front.
- If 4 receives a pass and is in a good shooting position, he may shoot at the goal. If this is not the case, 4 should start the piston movement again and the players repeat the course on the other side.
- And so on.

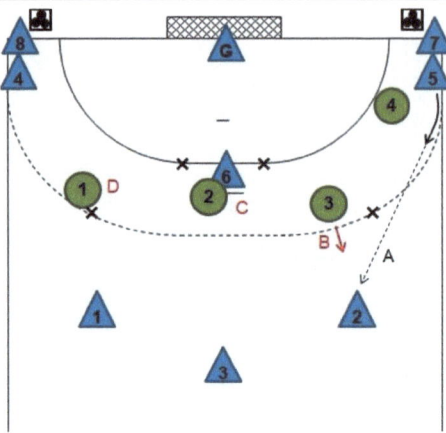

Figure 1 (right back player in ball possession)

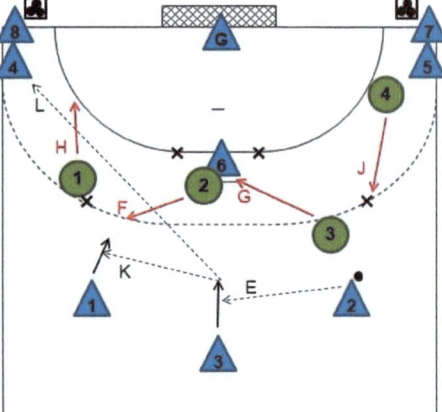

Figure 2 (change of defense positions during the pass)

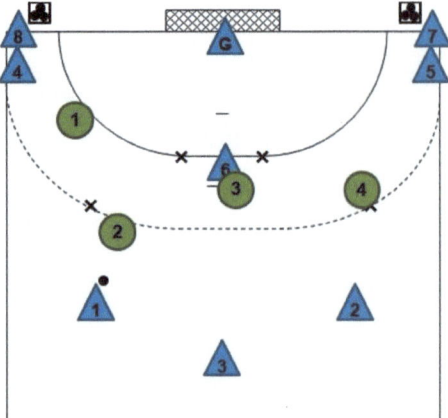

Figure 3 (left back player in ball possession)

⚠️ ①, ②, ③, and ④ should do the running moves in a highly dynamic manner. It is better to do only few, effective rounds than several ineffective rounds.

⚠️ ▲3 may also try to pass the ball to ▲4 directly (L). ① should always observe ▲3 and ▲4.

⚠️ The defense players simulate the running paths of the left/right back players and the two wing players in a 3-2-1 defense system. The exercise should initially be done without a defending center front/back player!

Special Handball Practice 1 – Step-by-step training of a 3-2-1 defense system

No.: Def. 5	Topic: 3-2-1 defense system		★★	90
Opening part		**Main part**		
X	Warm-up/Stretching		Offense/Individual		Jumping power
	Running exercise		Offense/Small groups	X	Sprint contest
X	Short game		Offense/Team		Goalkeeper
	Coordination		Offense/Series of shots		
	Coordination run	X	Defense/Individual	**Final part**	
	Strengthening		Defense/Small groups	X	Closing game
X	Ball familiarization	X	Defense/Team		Final sprint
X	Goalkeeper warm-up shooting		Athletics		
			Endurance		

Equipment required:
- 6 hoops
- 8 cones
- Ball box with sufficient number of handballs

No.: 5-1	Warm-up/Stretching	15	15

Course:
- The players crisscross the 6-meter zone (A).
- The coach's position defines the size of the field (keep changing) (B), in which the players are allowed to move.

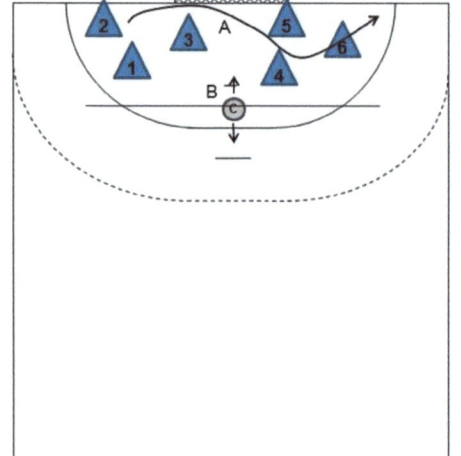

Instructions:
- Say "Hi" by exchanging a high-five with each approaching player.
- On command, run forward, backward or sidestep.
- Make a squat or a straight jump.

Competition:
Make two teams.
- Measure how long the players of one team need to push the players of the other team out of the 6-meter zone.
- Switch the tasks afterwards. Which team has pushed/forced all opponents out of the 6-meter zone fastest?

Variant:
- The players should dribble a ball during the task.

Afterwards, the players perform stretching exercises together; one player does an exercise which the others must do as well.

No.: 5-2	Short game	10	25

Course:

Two teams play team ball in the playing field. The teams may score a point as follows:
- The player receiving the pass must stand in a hoop with one foot (A).
- They do not get a point, if a player of the other team stands in the hoop as well (B).

Variants:
- The player must not only stand in the hoop, but also bounce the ball on the floor inside the hoop one time.

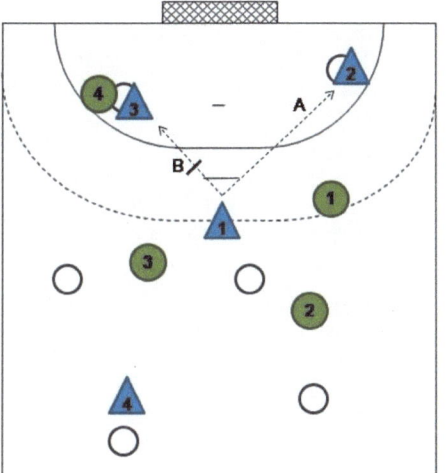

⚠ Make sure the distance between the hoops is not too long, so that the game becomes faster.

⚠ You need at least one more hoop than players per team, since otherwise, the task is too easy for the defending players.

| No.: 5-3 | Sprint contest | 5 | 30 |

Course:

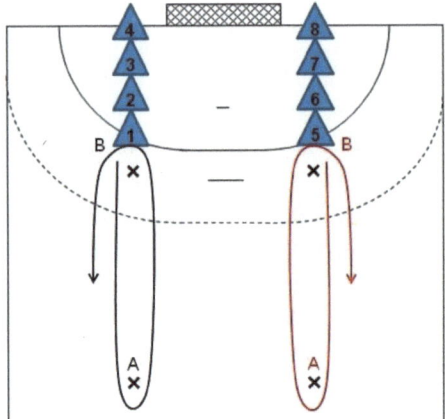

- 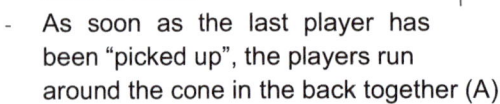 and start simultaneously on command and sprint to the cone in the back, run around it (A), and sprint back again.
- They take 2 (1) and 6 (5) by the hand (B) and sprint around the cone (A) and back as a pair.
- Afterwards, they take the third player by the hand and so on, until all players sprint around the cone hand in hand.
- As soon as the last player has been "picked up", the players run around the cone in the back together (A).
- Once they have come back,  let go and the other players sprint around the cone again (A).
- In each round and in reverse order, one of the players is allowed to let go at the starting position until only one player is left, who then sprints the last round alone.

The losing team must do push-ups or sit-ups, for example.

⚠ The competition is quite intense, as each player must sprint several rounds in a row.

⚠ Tactical running might be useful (due to the high physical strain, you cannot predict the winner before the end of the exercise).

Special Handball Practice 1 – Step-by-step training of a 3-2-1 defense system

| No.: 5-4 | **Ball familiarization** | 10 | 40 |

Course:

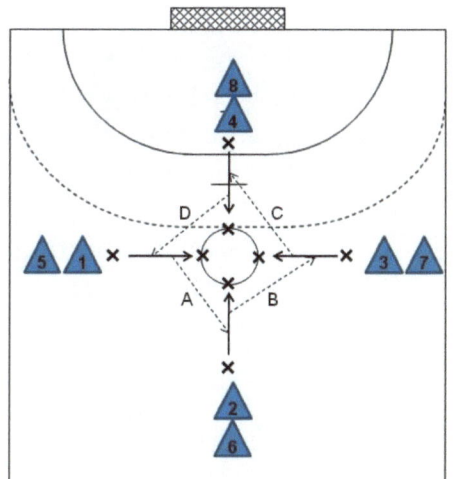

- ① makes a piston movement, passes (A) the ball to ② who also makes a piston movement and then passes the ball to (B) ③ who also makes a piston movement, and so on.
- After the dynamic piston movement, ① moves backward diagonally to the right and lines up behind ② ; ② lines up behind ③ , and so on.

Variants:

- ① runs a semicircle curve to ③ (on the opposite side) after the pass and lines up there. ② lines up behind ④ , ③ lines up behind ① , and ④ lines up behind ② .
- Passing path to the left/right, running path in opposite direction to the right/left.

| No.: 5-5 | **Goalkeeper warm-up shooting** | 10 | 50 |

Course:

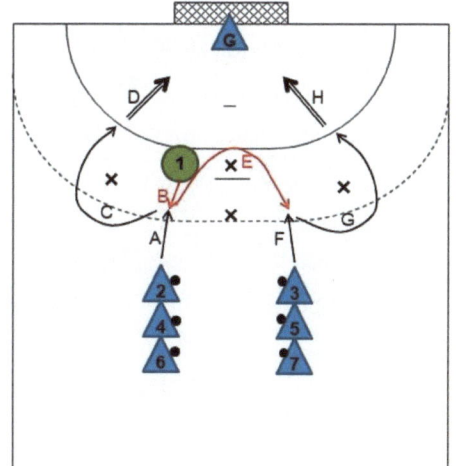

- ② makes a piston movement while holding the ball and feints a stem shot (A).
- ① makes a step forward and forces ② back a bit (B).
- After ② has been forced back, he changes the direction, dribbles around the cone (C), and finally shoots at the left side of the goal, as instructed (hands, top, bottom) (D).
- ① moves back, runs around the cone at the 6-meter line (E), and

then makes a step forward towards ③ who also makes a piston movement and feints a stem shot (F).
- ① pushes ③ back who subsequently dribbles around the cone (G), and finally shoots at the right side of the goal, as instructed (H).
- Afterwards, ④ starts. ① runs around the cone again and to the left side.
- And so on.

⚠ ① should push/force the attacking players back vigorously. Only after that, they should start running around the cone.

⚠ Change the defense player after each round.

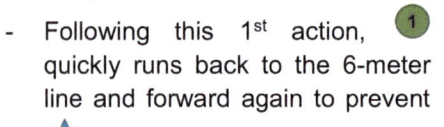

Course:

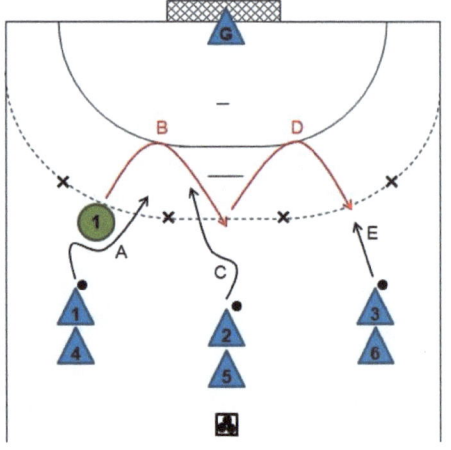

- ① starts a 1-on-1 action against ① with a ball (A), tries to get past him while dribbling, and to shoot at the goal.
- Following this 1st action, ① quickly runs back to the 6-meter line and forward again to prevent ② from breaking through (B).
- ② should quickly start his 1-on-1 action (C), but allow ① to get into the correct defending position.
- After the 2nd action, ① quickly runs back again to the 6-meter line and forward again (D) to prevent ③ from breaking through (E).
- Change the defense player afterwards, and so on (the new defense player must be ready so that there will be no break after the action of ①).

⚠ ① should hold the attacking players in front of him through quick legwork and by using his arms. The defense player must not tackle the attacking players but push/force them back.

⚠ He should first get the attacking player under control and then try to steal the ball.

| No.: 5-7 | Defense/Team | | 15 | 80 |

Basic position – Left back player is in ball possession (figure 1):

- ① stands offensively, next to ②.

- ② shields off the zone behind ①.

- ③ stands offensively, slightly orientated towards ①.

- ④ stands defensively, if ⑥ enters this area, ④ takes him over.

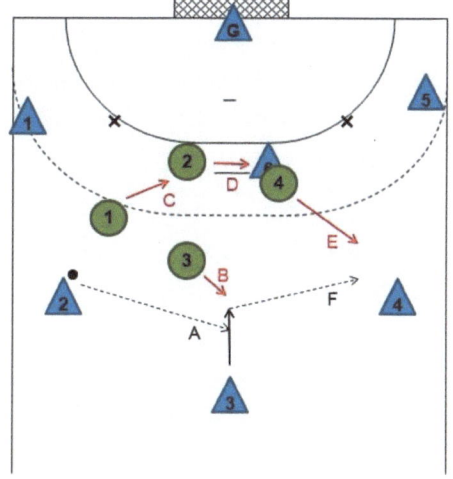

Figure 1

Course (figure 1):

- ① and ⑤ are the feeders/receivers.

- ② passes the ball into the running path of ③ (A):
  - ③ sidesteps towards the center, offensively orientated towards ③ (B).
  - ① sidesteps backward to the inner side (C).
  - ④ offensively steps forward (E).
  - ② moves along sidestepping and takes over the defense zone (⑥) of ④ (D).

- ③ passes the ball to ④ (F).

Basic course for the attacking players:

- The players pass the ball from ① to ⑤.
- ②, ③, and ④ try to break through 1-on-1 or to pass the ball to the pivot (⑥).
- The attacking players should increase the pressure on the defense players during the course of the exercise, in order to challenge the defense players more and more.
- Allow crossing moves and return passes during the further course of the drill.

Basic position – Right back player is in ball possession (figure 2):

- If 6 stays in the zone behind 4, 2 takes him over. 1 slightly moves to the inner side and covers the zone behind 3.
- If 6 moves to the left (G), 1 takes him over (H), and 2 covers the zone behind 4.

⚠ 1, 2, and 4 must communicate permanently with each other. Who is in charge of 6? How far should each defense player move along?

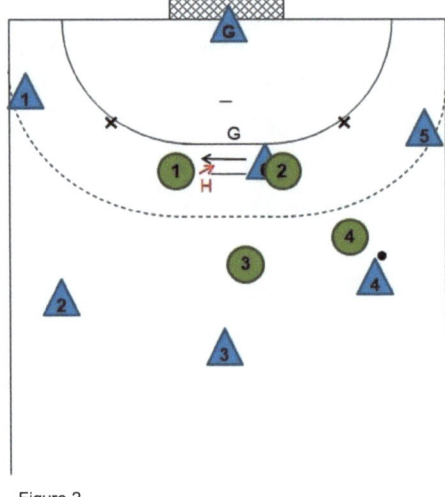

Figure 2

⚠ 6 should be rather static in the beginning. During the further course, however, he may change his position within the zone between the cones again and again.

No.: 5-8	Closing game	10	90

Course:
- Make two teams. Both teams play handball against each other.

Instructions:
- 3-2-1 defense system; the running paths should be reinforced in a game situation.

⚠ The defense players should communicate permanently and agree upon who is in charge of the respective attacking player.

⚠ The players should use their arms and hold their opponents in front of them.

No.: Def. 6	Topic: 3-2-1 defense system			★★	90
Opening part		**Main part**			
X	Warm-up/Stretching		Offense/Individual		Jumping power
	Running exercise		Offense/Small groups	X	Sprint contest
X	Short game		Offense/Team		Goalkeeper
	Coordination		Offense/Series of shots		
	Coordination run		Defense/Individual	**Final part**	
	Strengthening	X	Defense/Small groups		Closing game
X	Ball familiarization	X	Defense/Team		Final sprint
X	Goalkeeper warm-up shooting		Athletics		
			Endurance		

Equipment required:
- 2 large safety mats
- 6 cones
- 6 small vaulting boxes
- Ball box with sufficient number of handballs

No.: 6-1	Warm-up/Stretching	15	15

Course:
- The players crisscross the court for 5 minutes while doing different running variants (forward, backward, sidestep, hopping with/without arm rotation, and so on).
- Afterwards, two players each make a team and do the following exercises each for about 1 to 2 minutes:
    - The two players each stand face-to-face on one foot, keeping a distance of about half a meter. Through slight pushing with their arms, they try to unbalance each other (they first stand on the left, then on the right foot). If one of the players has to step on the floor with his second foot, the other player gets a point.
    - The players stand on the right and left side of a line and hold each other by one of their wrists. The players try to pull each other over the line (change arms during the course).

The players perform stretching exercises together.

No.: 6-2	Short game		10	25

Course:

Two teams play a rugby variant against each other. They should lay down the ball on the mat according to the following rules:
- They may pass the ball only to players who are running behind them.
- Dribbling is not allowed; however, the players may run freely and do any number of steps while holding the ball.
- Each team defends one mat.

⚠ This game is suitable ideally as a warm-up exercise of a training unit that focuses on defense (increases aggressiveness).

⚠ The defense players must help each other; only as a team they can stop an attacking player.

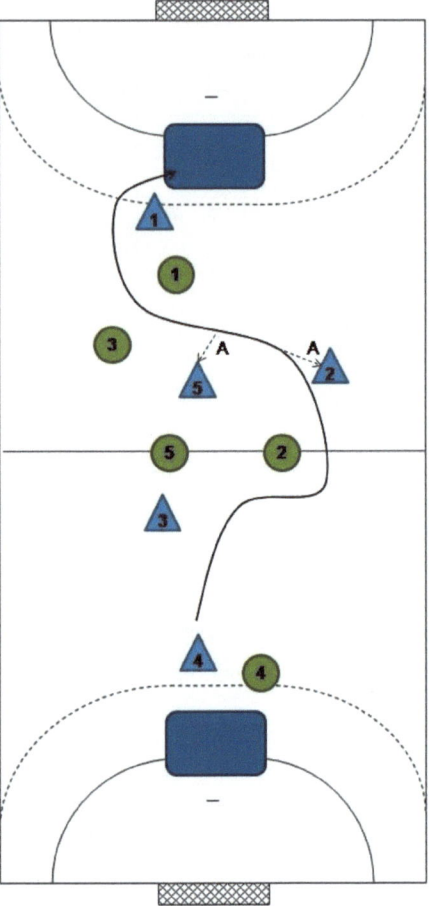

| No.: 6-3 | Ball familiarization | 10 | 35 |

Course:

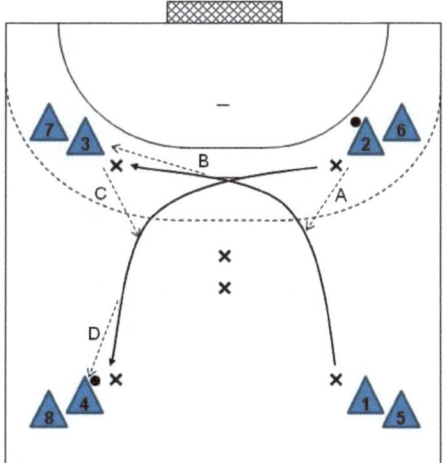

- 1 runs a curve without a ball and receives a pass from 2 (A).
- 1 passes to 3 (B) and lines up behind this group.
- As soon as 2 has passed the ball to 1, 2 starts to run a curve, receives a pass from 3 (C), passes the ball to 4 (D) and lines up there again.
- Afterwards, 3 starts, receives a pass from 4, passes the ball to 5, lines up there, and so on.

Variant:

- With two balls; 2 and 4 each have a ball and start simultaneously (high requirements on focusing!).

⚠ This exercise is intended to simulate quick passes during a fast break situation.

⚠ The players should start quickly and dynamically and pass the ball into the running path.

⚠ The players should increase their speed continuously.

| No.: 6-4 | Goalkeeper warm-up shooting | 10 | 45 |

Course:

- 3 starts the piston movement with a ball (A).
- 1 dynamically makes a step forward (B).
- 3 must pass the ball early enough (C) so that he is not interrupted by 1 (1 should clearly make a step forward towards 3, however).
- 2 receives a pass into his running path and shoots at the goal, as instructed (D) (to the left side from within the corridor).
- After his pass, 3 immediately moves back dynamically to his initial position (E).
- 1 dynamically moves backward and to the 6-meter line (F) in order to immediately make a step forward towards the piston movement path (G) of 4.
- 3 receives a pass into his running path and shoots at the goal, as instructed (to the right side from within the corridor) (H).

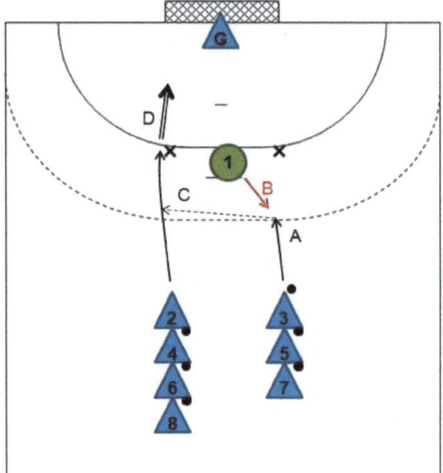

Figure 1

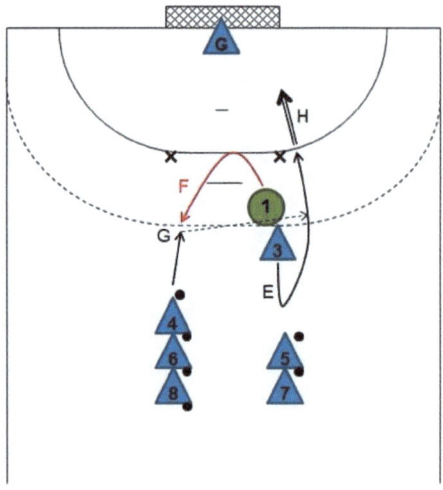

Figure 2

Variant:
- Jump shot.
- Shooting with the wrong foot in front.
- Sprinting to the center line immediately after the shot.

Special Handball Practice 1 – Step-by-step training of a 3-2-1 defense system

| No.: 6-5 | Sprint contest | 5 | 50 |

Course:

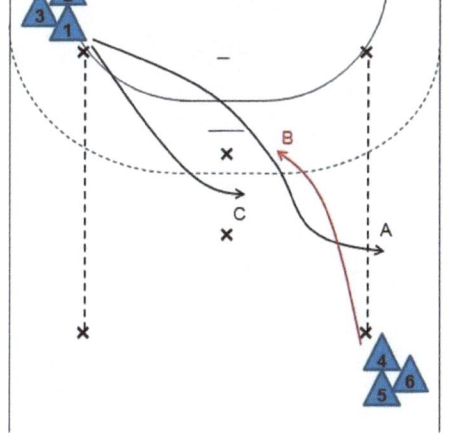

- ① tries to cross the opposite line on command, without being touched by ④ (A).
- ④ tries to catch ① and tag him (B).
- If ① manages to cross the line without being touched, he gets a point. If ④ touches him before, ④ gets a point.
- Afterwards, ② starts the same drill. Keep going until all players of the team have done the exercise. Switch tasks afterwards.
- Which team scores highest? The losing team must do push-ups or sit-ups.

Variant:

- If ① crosses the line directly (A), he gets one point. If ① takes the longer way through the cone goal and then crosses the line without being touched, he gets two points (C).

| No.: 6-6 | Defense/Small groups | 10 | 60 |

Course:

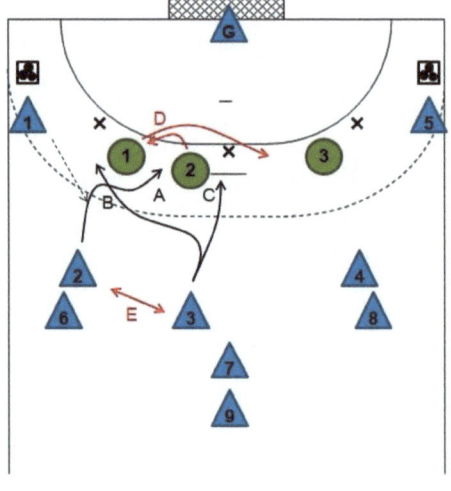

- ① plays the initial pass to ②.
- ② and ③ dynamically approach the defense line and together try to play off ① and ②:
  - ② performs a 1-on-1 action against ① (A).
  - ③ takes on the crossing of ② (B).
  - Alternatively, ③ runs along in parallel and tries to break through near the wing position (C).
- After the action, ① immediately runs to the right (D), and the players repeat the course on the other side (① and ③).
- ② moves along towards the wing position (D).
- ② and ③ switch positions after the crossing (E).
- And so on.

Change the defense players after a couple of minutes.

Basic course:
- If the two defense players manage to prevent a breakthrough, the two attacking players must do 10 push-ups.

⚠ The attacking players should not pass the ball over and over again in front of the defense line but rather immediately start a dynamic action.

⚠ The defense players should act vigorously while moving forward/to the side.

⚠ The center back (③, ⑦, and ⑨) should not stand directly in the center but rather a bit orientated to the left/right, depending on which side the attack is played.

Special Handball Practice 1 – Step-by-step training of a 3-2-1 defense system

No.: 6-7	Defense/Team		10	70

Course:

- 5 passes to 2 (A).
- 3 makes a step forward and attacks 2 (B).
- 2 covers 6 in parallel (C).
- 1 simultaneously stands offensively at the 9-meter line, between 1 and 4 (D).
- 2 passes the ball into the running path of 3 (E).
- 3 passes the ball into the running path of 1 (K).
- 2 dynamically makes a step forward and attacks 1 (F) in parallel.
- 3 takes over 6 in parallel (G).
- 1 dynamically runs to the wing position and blocks 4 (H).
- Figure 3 shows the positions when the left back player is in ball possession.
- If 4 receives a pass and is in a good shooting position, he may shoot at the goal. If this is not the case, 4 should start the piston movement again and the players repeat the course on the other side.
- And so on.

Figure 1 (right back player in ball possession)

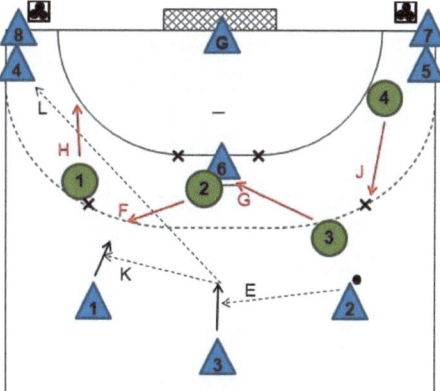

Figure 2 (change of defense positions during the pass)

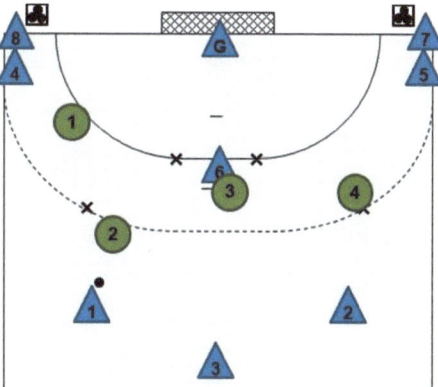

Figure 3 (left back player in ball possession)

⚠ ①, ②, ③, and ④ should do the running moves in a highly dynamic manner. It is better to do only few, effective rounds than several ineffective rounds.

⚠ ▲3 may also try to pass the ball to ▲4 directly. ① should always observe ▲3 and ▲4.

⚠ The defense players simulate the running paths of the left/right back players and the two wing players in a 3-2-1 defense system. The exercise should initially be done without a defending center front/back player!

No.: 6-8	Defense/Team		20	90

Introduction:
- Combination of the individual exercises to implement a complete 3-2-1 defense system.

Ball possession left wing player:
- ① direct, fixed coverage of ▲1 who is in ball possession.
- ② stands offensively, orientated towards ▲1.
- ④ covers the zone behind ②. If ▲6 stands in the zone behind ②, ④ takes him over.
- ③ stands offensively, orientated towards the zone between ▲2 and ▲3.
- ⑤ takes over ▲6, if he stands on the right side (as shown in the example; figure 1).
- ⑥ stands semi-offensively; he should keep in mind diagonal passes (A) from ▲1 to ▲5 and then move towards the wing position (B).

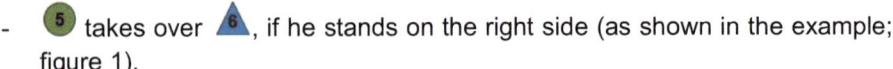

Figure 1

Special Handball Practice 1 – Step-by-step training of a 3-2-1 defense system

Ball possession left back player:

- ② offensively makes a step forward towards ▲2.
- ③ stands offensively, orientated towards the zone between ▲2 and ▲3.
- ④ covers the zone behind ②. If ▲6 stands in the zone behind ②, ④ takes him over.
- ⑤ takes over ▲6, if he stands on the right side (as shown in the example; figure 2) in order to prevent a pass (C).
- ⑥ stands offensively, with the objective to prevent the parallel piston movement of ▲4 (F). However, he should also keep direct passes (D) to ▲5 in mind and then move towards the wing position (E).

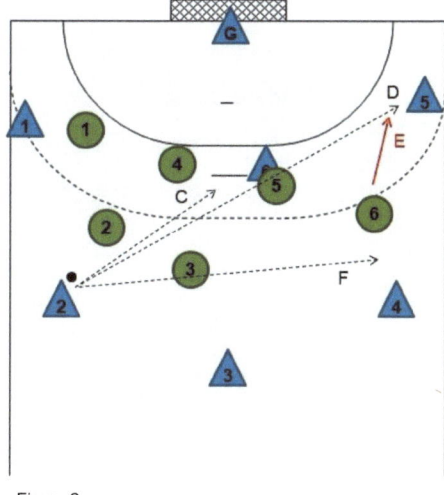

Figure 2

Ball possession center back player:

- ③ offensively makes a step forward towards ▲3.
- ⑤ makes a step forward in direction of ▲4.
- ② keeps his offensive position next to ▲2.
- ② and ⑤ should keep in mind that ▲2 and ▲4 might enter the zone (crossing) (H).
- ① and ⑥ keep their positions and should keep in mind that ▲1 and ▲5 might enter the zone, i.e. prevent them from doing so (G).
- ④ takes over ▲6 and stays with him until he is able to hand him over. He should be aware that the pivot might leave the zone at any time (J).

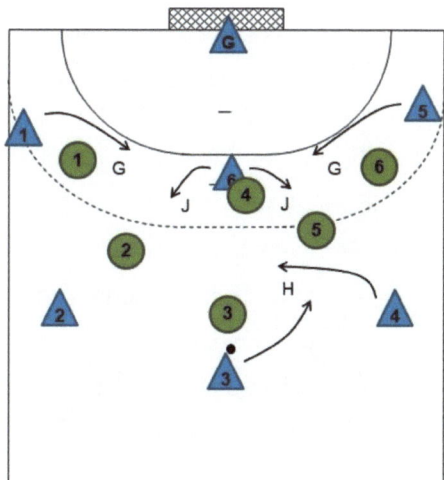

Figure 3

Ball possession right back player:

- ⑤ offensively makes a step forward towards ▲4.
- ③ stands offensively, orientated towards the zone between ▲3 and ▲4.
- ④ covers the zone behind ⑤. If ▲6 stands in the zone behind ⑤, ④ takes him over.
- ② takes over ▲6, if he stands on the left side (as shown in the example; figure 4) in order to prevent a pass (N).
- ① stands offensively, with the objective to prevent the parallel piston movement of ▲2 (M). However, he should also keep direct passes (K) to ▲1 in mind and then move towards the wing position (L).

Figure 4

Ball possession right wing player:

- ⑥ direct, fixed coverage of ▲5 who is in ball possession.
- ⑤ stands offensively, orientated towards ▲5.
- ④ covers the zone behind ⑤. If ▲6 stands in the zone behind ⑤, ④ takes him over.
- ③ stands offensively, orientated towards the zone between ▲3 and ▲4.
- ② takes over ▲6, if he stands on the left side (as shown in the example; figure 5).
- ① stands semi-offensively; he should keep in mind diagonal passes (O) from ▲5 to ▲1 and then move towards the wing position (P).

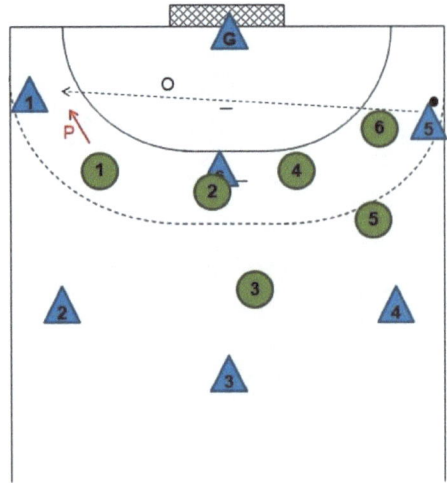

Figure 5

Basic course for the attacking players:
- The attacking players pass the ball from the left to the right side and back again.
- They do this very slow in the beginning, so that the defense players are able to assign themselves to their respective opponent.
- 🔺6 initially keeps his position.

- The players should increase the passing speed after a couple of minutes.
- 🔺6 should move within the zone between the left back and right back player.
- The players now also may cross.

⚠️ The defense players should communicate permanently and clearly agree upon which defense player is assigned to which attacking player. ②, ④, and ⑤ must agree upon how to hand over 🔺6, in particular.

6. About the editor

JÖRG MADINGER, born in Heidelberg (Germany) in 1970

July 2014 (further training): 3-day coaching workshop: "Basic components of goalkeeper training", held by the **German Handball Association (Deutscher Handballbund, DHB)**
Lecturers: Michael Neuhaus, Renate Schubert, Marco Stange, Norbert Potthoff, Olaf Gritz, Andreas Thiel, Henning Fritz

May 2014 (further training): 3-day coaching further training during the VELUX EHF Final4, held by the **German Handball Coaching Association (Deutsche Handball Trainer Vereinigung, DHTV)/DHB**
Lecturers: Jochen Beppler (DHB coach), Christian vom Dorff (DHB referee), Mark Dragunski (coach of TuSeM Essen, Germany), Klaus-Dieter Petersen (DHB coach), Manolo Cadenas (coach of the Spanish national team)

May 2013 (further training): 3-day coaching further training during the VELUX EHF Final4, held by the **DHTV/DHB**
Lecturers: Prof. Dr. Carmen Borggrefe (University of Stuttgart, Germany), Klaus-Dieter Petersen (DHB coach), Dr. Georg Froese (sports psychologist), Jochen Beppler (DHB base camp coach), Carsten Alisch (young talents' hockey coach)

Since July 2012: A-License, DHB

Since February 2011: Handball club trainings, coaching (training and competitive areas)

November 2011: Foundation of the Handball Specialist Publishing Company (Handball Fachverlag) (handall-uebungen.de, Handball Practice and Special Handball Practice)

May 2009: Foundation of the handball online platform handball-uebungen.de

2008-2010: Youth coordinator and youth coach, SG Leutershausen (Germany)

Since 2006: B-License

Editor's note
In 1995, a friend convinced me to join him in coaching a handball youth team (male, under 13 years of age).

This was the beginning of my career as a team handball coach. Ever since I enjoyed working as a coach and had high requirements concerning my exercises. Soon, the standard pool of exercises wasn't enough for me anymore and I started to modify and develop drills myself.

Today, I coach a broad range of youth and adult teams with different performance levels and adjust my training units to the individual needs of the teams.

A few years ago, I started selling my exercises and drills online at handball-uebungen.de. Since, in handball training, there is a tendency towards a general athletic training that focuses on coordination work – especially in the training of youth teams –, a large number of my games and exercises can be applied to other sports as well.

Get inspired by the various game concepts, be creative, and rely on your own experiences!

Yours sincerely,
Jörg Madinger

7. Further reference books published by DV Concept

From warm-up to handball team play – 75 exercises for every handball training unit

By making your training units more diverse, you can increase the players' motivation, since you consistently offer new approaches to improve and refine familiar movement sequences. In this book, you will find inspiring exercises you can apply during each phase of your everyday team handball training – from warm-up and goalkeeper warm-up shooting to the common contents of the main phase and the closing games. Each exercise is illustrated and described in an easy, comprehensible manner. Specific notes give you tips on what you need to be aware of.

This book deals with the following key subjects:

Warm-up:
- Basic warm-up
- Short warm-up games
- Sprint contests
- Coordination
- Ball familiarization
- Goalkeeper warm-up shooting

Basic exercises, basic play, and target play:
- Offense/series of shots
- General offense
- Fast throw-off
- 1st and 2nd wave
- Defensive action
- Closing games
- Endurance

At the end of this book, you will find an entire methodological training unit. The objective of this training unit is to improve shooting and quick decision-making under pressure.

Minihandball training and handball training for young kids (5 training units)

Minihandball training and handball training for kids is different from handball training for older players and considerably different from handball training for competitive players. During their first contact with "handball", kids should be familiarized with the ball in a playful way. They should be taught that being active, doing sports, playing together, and even playing against each other is fun.

This book contains a short introduction to handball for kids and young children and its special characteristics as well as example exercises which help to make your training units interesting and more diverse.

Following this, there are five complete training units of different difficulty levels that focus on the basic handball techniques (dribbling, passing, catching, shooting, and defending in a game with opponents). The kids are playfully introduced to the subsequent handball-specific basics. At the same time, particular attention is payed to general physical experience and the development of coordination skills.

The exercises are illustrated and described in an easy, comprehensible manner. They can be immediately integrated in every training unit. By using the given training variants, you can easily adjust the difficulty level of the training units to the respective target group. The variants should also encourage you to modify and further develop the exercises to make each training unit a new and more diverse experience for the children.

Passing and catching while moving – 60 exercises for each handball training unit

Passing and catching are two basic handball techniques which must be trained and improved continuously. These 60 practical exercises offer you various options to train passing and catching in a challenging and diverse manner. The exercises particularly focus on improving passing and catching skills even during highly dynamic movements. The drills therefore combine new running paths and movements similar to real game situations.

The exercises are illustrated and described in an easy, comprehensible manner. They can be immediately integrated in every training unit. Various difficulty and complexity levels allow for adjustment of the passing and catching drills to each age group.

Effective goalkeeper warm-up shooting – 60 exercises for every handball unit

Goalkeeper warm-up shooting is essential for almost every training unit. These 60 warm-up shooting exercises provide you with a variety of ideas to make the warm-up shooting challenging and diverse, both for the goalkeepers and the field players. The exercises particularly focus on improving the players' dynamics even during the warm-up shooting.

The exercises are illustrated and described in an easy, comprehensible manner. They can be immediately integrated in every training unit. Whether you combine the exercises with additional coordination drills or use them as an introduction to the main part – various difficulty levels allow for adjustment of the warm-up shooting to each training unit and age group.

Competitive games for your everyday handball training – 60 exercises for each age-group

Handball needs quick and correct decisions in each game situation. This can be trained playfully and diversely through handball-specific games. These 60 exercises are divided into seven categories and train the playing skills.

The book deals with the following subjects:
- Team ball variants
- Team play with different targets
- Tag games
- Sprint and relay race games
- Ball throwing and transportation games
- Games from other types of sports
- Complex closing game variants

The exercises are illustrated and described in an easy, comprehensible manner. They can be immediately integrated in every training unit. Various difficulty levels, additional notes, and possible variations allow for adjustment to each age group.

Paperback from the Handball Practice series (Handball Praxis) (five training units each)

Handball Practice 11 – Extensive and diverse athletics training

For further reference and e-books visit us at:
www.handball-uebungen.de

www.ingramcontent.com/pod-product-compliance
Lightning Source LLC
Chambersburg PA
CBHW041803160426
43191CB00001B/26